Maya Glyphs

Cover Carved lintel with glyphic text, recording blood-letting ceremony of Na Wak Tun, probable consort of Bird Jaguar III, lord of Yaxchilan. AD 755. H. 80 cm. British Museum.

Frontispiece The Fenton Vase, possibly from Nebaj, Guatemala; a scene of tribute from the Late Classic period. Diam 17.2 cm. British Museum.

Maya Glyphs

S. D. Houston

University of California Press/British Museum

Acknowledgements

I am grateful to Dr George Stuart of the National Geographic Society for Figures 7 and 23; to Otis Imboden of the same institution goes credit for Figure 5. Mr Ian Graham of the Maya Corpus Project, Peabody Museum, Harvard University, kindly supplied Figures 4, 6 and 10, and Dr Eric Gibson provided the rendering in Figure 13, drawn and inked by Dr Peter Mathews. Four illustrations come from published or soon-to-be-published sources. Figure 14 is taken from a rubbing in V. Fialko's 'El marcador de juego de pelota de Tikal', in *Primer Simposio Mundial sobre Epigrafía Maya* (Guatemala City, 1987). Figure 17 is from N. Hellmuth's *Monster und Menschen in der Maya-Kunst* (Graz, 1987). Figure 18, of the dancing jaguar, appeared first in M. Coe's *Lords of the Underworld* (Princeton, 1978), and Figure 19 is drawn from Martine Fettweis-Vienot's Paris thesis, *Les Peintures Murales Postclassiques du Quintana Roo, Mexique*, soon to be issued as a book.

University of California Press
Berkeley and Los Angeles, California

© 1989 The Trustees of the British Museum

Third impression 1996

Front cover design by Grahame Dudley

Printed in Great Britain

Library of Congress Cataloguing-in-Publication Data

Houston, Stephen D.
    Maya Glyphs/S. D. Houston
        p.   cm. – (Reading the past; v. 7)
    Bibliography: p.
    Includes index.
    ISBN 0–520–06771–1 (alk. paper): $7.95 (est.)
    1. Mayas—Writing.   2. Mayas-Antiquities.
    3. Indians of Mexico—Writing.   4. Indians of
    Central America—Writing.   5. Indians of Mexico—
    Antiquities.   6. Indians of Central America—
    Antiquities.
    I. Title   II. Series
    P1435.3.P6H67   1989   89-50219
    497' .4—oc19   CIP

ISBN 0-520-06771-1

Contents

Preface

The decipherment of Maya hieroglyphs is at an exciting point. Only now are epigraphers achieving a detailed understanding of scribal art and society. This book will have been successful if it communicates a fraction of the energy and momentum of the field, and if the reader comes to experience firsthand one of the last great decipherments.

But there is also a challenge in presenting much that is new and only partly published. As a result, a book of this sort owes much to the generosity of colleagues, particularly David Stuart, who has given freely of his deep knowledge of Maya glyphs. I am grateful, too, for the perceptive comments of Norman Hammond and Karl Taube, who have read the manuscript carefully. Readers should understand that full justifications for decipherments must appear elsewhere, in more technical publications. For those wishing to know more there is a short bibliographical note at the end of the book.

Glyphic transcriptions require some explanation. Literal renderings appear in bold type, with capital letters marking word signs, or 'logographs', and lower-case

letters denoting phonetic elements. Transliterations that reproduce actual Maya words are in italic. Thus,

can be written in three ways: **to-k'(a)** (a transcription); *tok'* (a transliteration); and 'flint' (a translation). The orthography is taken from Alfredo Barrera V.'s *Diccionario Maya Cordemex*, the *O.E.D.* of Yucatec Maya.

Two last points. As an adjective, 'Mayan' refers to language and writing. 'Maya' applies to all other features of this people, including their archaeology. None the less, 'Maya' is used throughout so as not to confuse the reader with pedantic details. Also linguists may chafe at the use of 'tense' rather than the more correct 'aspect', and of 'past tense' instead of 'perfective aspect'. To them my apologies, yet sometimes precision, and daunting technical vocabulary, must be sacrificed for the sake of readability.

1   Roll-out of scene of tribute on the Fenton Vase illustrated on p. 1.

1

Discovery and Decipherment

All writing is used to convey information, and Maya glyphs are no exception. From just after the time of Christ until a century or two after the Spanish conquest, the Maya of Central America and Mexico recorded highly esoteric knowledge in one of the most complex scripts ever devised. The story of its decipherment, still very much in progress, reveals mistakes, false starts and misconceptions; but there is also insight, patient scholarship and luck, leading to what we now know of the language, history and culture of an important pre-Columbian civilisation.

The first Europeans to see Maya glyphs were Spanish priests and soldiers, who marvelled at the 'great curiosity and assiduity' of the signs. Only a few Maya could read them, however, and it was not long before native documents were consigned to the bonfire or, more usually, to the neglect and oblivion of official archives. The glyphs were too much a part of pagan belief to be compatible with missionising Christianity, and too much the instruments of a native élite to survive long in Colonial America.

Before disappearing entirely, or being reduced to the meaningless squiggles of the eighteenth century, a few signs made their way into Spanish treatises of the early Colonial period. Typically, such works contained unperceptive, incomplete or misleading descriptions, although there was one notable exception: the 'Account of the Things of Yucatan' by Fray Diego de Landa of the Franciscan Order.

There are few richer sources on the Maya. Comprehensive, accurate and penetrating, Landa's 'Account' contains a useful description of Maya calendrical signs and a mysterious 'alphabet', which proved eventually to be one of the keys to decipherment. But this came only much later: Landa's manuscript languished in obscurity for nearly 300 years, and it was not until the nineteenth century that Maya glyphs again attracted serious attention.

In the intervening years the script degenerated. Native scribes began to rely exclusively on European script, and glyphs became doubly dead, being lost both to native tradition and to Western scholarship. However, the gloom was not to last. The Enlightenment brought with it political change, which lifted restrictions on travel in Mexico and Central America, and also heightened curiosity about 'natural man', including the native peoples of the New World. Expeditions sponsored by the Colonial authorites brought forth reports of cities concealed under jungle, and with them crude drawings of inscriptions carved in stone. At the same time a Maya screen-fold manuscript, the Dresden Codex, came to light in the Royal Library of Dresden. Alexander von Humboldt published it in part, but, as George Stuart of the National Geographic Society has shown, it remained for Constantine Rafinesque, an American naturalist, to connect the codex and inscriptions with the Maya. Earlier descriptions had labelled the texts as 'Aztec' or 'Mexican'.

Typically, the enthusiasts of the time were eccentric, mendacious and more than willing to make exaggerated claims. There were few who could contradict them. But with greater interest came more competent and systematic exploration, in which John Lloyd Stephens, a noted American travel writer, and his English artist

2 Copan Altar Q. AD 763;
etched by A.L. Dick from a drawing
by F. Catherwood.

Frederick Catherwood figured prominently. Stephens and Catherwood visited
Central America and Mexico in two separate trips, between 1839 and 1842. The
accounts of their travels were bestsellers of the day. Stephens described Maya ruins
in stylish and lively prose, and Catherwood, alone among his contemporaries, suc-
ceeded in reproducing the baroque shapes of Maya glyphs and art. Some of
Stephens's remarks were far-sighted. He concluded that monuments depicted
rulers and that glyphs recited royal history. Nearly 120 years passed before these
suggestions were taken up and confirmed.

Progress was delayed by the poor knowledge of Maya texts and languages. By its nature decipherment depends on the availability of inscriptions; without a sufficient number ideas cannot be tested and confirmed; and without some understanding of grammar and vocabulary there can be little hope of using a modern language to explain its ancestor. This deficiency began gradually to be remedied by methodical search in libraries, which were rather easier to visit then remote ruins. A French cleric, Brasseur de Bourbourg, found no fewer than five key manuscripts, including Landa's manuscript, a Colonial dictionary and a second Maya codex, in Madrid. The discovery in Paris of a third codex supplemented this rich haul.

The tools for decipherment were almost in hand. At this point the caretaker of the Dresden Codex, Ernst Förstemann, applied his considerable intellect to unravelling the Maya calendrical systems. His were not the first discoveries, but he integrated prior findings with his own to achieve stunning breakthroughs. Förstemann explained how the calendar worked, emphasising its vigesimal (base twenty) character with respect to the so-called Long Count, a place-notational

3   Alfred Maudslay (1850–1931).

system recording time elapsed since a base date in the fourth millennium BC. He also identified the glyphs of the Long Count and recognised a distinctive feature of Maya writing: the 'head variants', or glyphs with animal or human faces, that were equivalent to more common signs.

Naturally, most of Förstemann's work relied on his keen understanding of the codices; but he began also to interpret some texts on stone monuments. This was an important step, which followed directly on work by the American Cyrus Thomas, who some years earlier had compared the Madrid codex with a Maya text in the possession of the National Museum in Washington and established reading in pairs of columns. Such studies demonstrated that Maya writing was an integral system: scholars could not study monuments of codices without taking account of their fundamental similarities.

The focus on monumental inscriptions became particularly apparent with the publications of the Englishman Alfred Maudslay. In a discipline known for its large personalities Maudslay represented something different: he was indefatigable, patient, meticulous and, above all, modest. His documentation of site plans and inscriptions of the most important sites in the Maya lowlands were unsurpassed until the second half of the twentieth century. Maudslay's only rival was the German scholar Teobert Maler, an irascible, rather embittered person whose main contribution were site plans and very fine photographs of monuments that are now eroded.

Maudslay encouraged others to use his work. Of these the most notable was Joseph Goodman, who gave Mark Twain his first job as a journalist on the *The Territorial Enterprise* of Virginia City, Nevada. Goodman has long been a controversial figure. Some believe he plagiarised Förstemann, an accusation that is still difficult to evaluate. But this should not detract from his decipherments: he identified the head variants for numerals and found much of importance in Maya calendrics. Indeed, his is the 'correlation' – the linkage between absolute dates in Maya and European calendars – that, with modifications, continues to prevail.

Goodman and Förstemann's emphasis on calendrics may seem single-minded today, when so much else is known, yet it did produce results according to its own rigorous methods. To some it was the only viable approach. During the next sixty years scholars continued to increase their understanding of Maya chronology, although increasingly with support from institutions rather than private benefactors.

One great figure of the period was the American archaeologist Sylvanus Griswold Morley, who devoted much of his life to documenting inscriptions, or 'bringing home the epigraphic bacon', as he liked to put it. His decipherments now seem somewhat negligible, his photographs and drawings well below the standards achieved by Maudslay and Maler. But there was much more to this energetic and affable explorer, and Maya epigraphy would have been the poorer without him. Morley managed to convince the Carnegie Institution of Washington to support a long-term programme of research on Maya civilisation. Ambitious excavations began at the sites of Chichen Itza, Copan, Quirigua and Uaxactun, as well as myriad smaller sites. As shown by his monumental *Inscriptions of the Peten*, truly Morley 'brought home the bacon'.

12

4 S.G. Morley at Copan, *c*.1912.

Some criticised the Carnegie programme as barren and narrow, without any real anthropological purpose. There was truth to this judgement, although it was unduly harsh. The programme was designed to study a civilisation in its entirety, from historical, biological, astronomical, linguistic, artistic and archaeological perspectives. To accomplish this goal it published work by the finest minds of the generation: John Teeple on Maya astronomy, Hermann Beyer on the difficult inscriptions of Yucatan, and many others on a variety of topics.

Both Teeple and Beyer made important, if dramatically different, contributions. Teeple was an engineer who travelled a great deal. During his trips he pondered the glyphs accompanying the Initial Series, a form of the Long Count appearing at the beginning of many monumental texts. Teeple determined that these signs related in precise ways to the lunar calendar. He also proposed the notorious 'determinant' theory which, by its brilliance, took nearly thirty years to disprove, blinding scholars to the true nature of the script.

Teeple noticed, as had others, that Maya inscriptions contained more than a single date. He proposed that some dates functioned as 'determinants': that is, they indicated or 'determined' the gain of a Maya year of 365 days over the true solar year of 365.2422 in the period since the predicated beginning of the current Maya era, in 3113 BC. Thus, at the Long Count date of 9.17.0.0.0 (AD 771) the Maya year was 210 days ahead of the solar year. By subtracting or adding this amount one arrived at a second and third date, which were the determinants of 9.17.0.0.0. Virtually all Teeple's determinants now appear to be historical dates.

5   Sir Eric Thompson (1898–1975).

Unlike Teeple, whose theories were much acclaimed at the time, Beyer was almost ahead of his day. Rather than focusing on calendrical signs, he concentrated on the mysterious non-calendrical signs, paying special attention to the inscriptions of Chichen Itza in northern Yucatan. By careful comparisons he established the existence of parallel sequences of signs, some of which seemed to be equivalent, though of different form. This method of determining patterns of alternation – of discerning the *structure* of the writing – lies at the very heart of modern epigraphic work. Beyer's contemporaries did not know quite what to make of it, although at least one person praised its originality.

This was an Englishman, J. Eric S. (later Sir Eric) Thompson. Like other British Mayanists Thompson spent most of his productive working life in the United States, where there was strong institutional support for New World archaeology. He was fantastically prolific, with well over 250 publications to his credit, including papers on linguistics, archaeology and ethnology. Between 1940 and 1960 he completely dominated Maya epigraphy, and his *Maya Hieroglyphic Writing*, published nearly forty years ago, remains a basic text.

Thompson's work is thematically consistent. He continually stressed the flexibility of Maya script. Signs were apparently used not so much for their meaning as their sound, so that the glyph for 'tree', read *te*, occurred in contexts without the slightest connection to trees. This was a variation of the rebus principle, in which hieroglyphs of similar sound but different meaning alternate freely. (In English rebus the picture of a human eye could mean either the pronoun 'I' or quite literally 'eye'.) When combined with Beyer's approach, rebus helped establish chains of equivalent signs, advancing epigraphy more than perhaps any other method.

A second theme of Thompson's work is a reliance on the ethnographic record and on Colonial Maya documents, which deal with history as recurring prophecy. Thompson gradually developed a highly abstract view of the writing and the society that used it. To Thompson Maya rulers were peaceful priests given to philosophical speculation about the nature of time and prophecy. Their understanding of such esoteric phenomena enabled them to predict astronomical cycles, presumably to the astonishment and appreciation of their underlings.

Thompson's reputation is secure. Yet his notion of impersonal history was for the most part swept away by the work of Heinrich Berlin and Tatiana Proskouriakoff, who demonstrated that the script recorded biography. There had been some glimmerings of this before. Stephens and, at first, Morley believed the inscriptions to be historical but failed to prove their assertions.

Berlin's was the first breakthrough. He showed that some glyphs were tightly associated with particular sites; and if the precise meaning was uncertain, it seemed clear at least that the signs were emblematic, referring possibly to place names, tutelary deities or dynasties – hence their name 'Emblem glyphs'. In later work Berlin identified royal names at Palenque. His work consistently showed the same emphasis on structure as Beyer's.

6   Tatiana Proskouriakoff (1909–85).

Proskouriakoff entered Maya archaeology as an architect. Her reconstruction drawings of Maya cities are still esteemed for their fidelity to excavation data, but her greatest contribution came through her study of the formal characteristics of Maya art. This research placed emphasis on the correct dating of monuments, since this allowed her to chart changes in artistic style. The eventual result was wholly unexpected. In addition to artistic phases she found a marked pattern of dates at certain sites. The periods thus delimited corresponded closely to human lifespans. At the beginning were probable birth glyphs, followed some twenty-five years later by accession glyphs. The periods closed with signs for death.

Thompson gracefully conceded his error but chose not to incorporate the discoveries into his own work, which became increasingly devoted to the codices, where augury did indeed play a role. Berlin and Proskouriakoff continued work until their deaths, and their legacy survived in the research of a burgeoning number of epigraphers. Today the historical outline of Maya civilisation is fairly clear, and the 'historical hypothesis', which detected history in the inscriptions, has become proven fact.

Epigraphic controversy had by this time shifted to another issue: phoneticism in Maya script. The debate began with the discovery of Landa's 'alphabet'. Despite repeated attempts, it failed utterly to explain glyphs in the way Landa described. Cyrus Thomas's case was especially poignant. He had made his name not only with his epigraphy but by debunking the 'Lost Moundbuilder' theory, which held that mounds in the American South and Midwest were the work of Israelites rather than native North Americans. Thomas was inclined, then, to see complex features in another native achievement, the Maya script; but his arguments were weak, forcing him eventually to repudiate the 'alphabet'.

The problem was that Landa's list was mislabelled. Very soon after its discovery scholars recognised that Landa had recorded *syllables* rather than letters; thus, having elicited 'b', *be* in Spanish, Landa got the glyph for *be*. Clearly this was no alphabet.

At stake was an important principle. Thompson insisted that all glyphs had to be at least a morpheme, a unit that could not be divided into smaller meaningful parts. Phoneticism implied the existence of smaller units, particularly sounds, which could be joined together regardless of their origin in identifiable images. A strong advocate of this view was Benjamin Whorf, a linguist of some distinction. Whorf argued that signs could be reduced to even smaller parts, a hook indicating one sound, doubled lines another. Although his particular argument was easily refuted, the idea did not do away.

The phonetic breakthrough came in the early 1950s. A young Soviet linguist, Yurii Knorosov, presented his ideas in a series of papers, some couched in Marxist-Leninist jargon. This alone ensured a frosty reception in the West. Worse still his method was not laid out very clearly, exposing him to ready attack by Thompson and others.

Knorosov believed the alphabet had been completely misinterpreted. Rather it was a *syllabary*, a collection of consonant/vowel combinations. When joined, such syllables formed words consisting of consonant + vowel + consonant; and since few Mayan words ended in vowels, the final letter was dropped. Knorosov

7 Bishop Landa's 'alphabet'.

proposed that the dropped or 'dead' vowel accorded with the first one, a principle he termed 'synharmony'. This was important for revealing the vowel of the second syllable in a phonetic spelling.

The test for Knorosov came from the codices, the ideal laboratories for epigraphy. Most codical glyphs accompany scenes of animals and gods in a wide variety of acts: offering, conversation, drilling, copulation, etc. Presumably the glyphs explained and labelled the images.

Knorosov began by taking a sign from Landa, *ku*, and applying it to a spelling for 'turkey', *kutz* in Yucatec Maya. *Ku* was the first of the two glyphs. The second, though not in Landa's list, was probably *tzu* (synharmony dictated the vowel). Knorosov then turned to the two glyphs for 'dog'. The first glyph was the hypothetic *tzu*, the second Landa's *lu*. *Tzul*, or *tzu-l (u)* as the Maya would have spelt it, was an old Yucatec word for 'dog'.

8
A phonetic spelling for *kutz,* 'turkey', from the Dresden Codex, *c.* AD 1250.

It took a surprisingly long time for the theory to be accepted. Knorosov himself must be blamed for presenting weak evidence along with the strong, but he was well served by his supporters. David Kelley argued cogently in his favour, providing the decipherment of *k'a-k'u-pa-ka-l(a)* or 'fiery shield' in the inscriptions of Chichen Itza. A momentous find, the name was documented in Colonial sources as a leader of the Itza people and the founder of an important city. Interest quickened: Proskouriakoff sponsored a translation of Knorosov's work, and Michael Coe highlighted phoneticism in his introduction to Maya archaeology.

9
A phonetic spelling of *k'ak' u pakal*, from Chichen Itza, AD 880.

An important result of Knorosov's decipherments was a greater attention to the language of the Maya. Linguists such as Floyd Lounsbury began to reveal nuances in the script not readily apparent to epigraphers, who largely came to the discipline from archaeology. Maya glyphic grammar, sketched briefly by Whorf in the 1930s, became more accessible with this approach: verbs were evidently written first, followed by what appeared to be subjects. The decipherment of pronouns and aspect tense particles – indicating when an event happened – penetrated even further into the language of the ancient Maya.

Such attention to detail necessitated better drawings of inscriptions. With only a few exceptions standards had dropped since Maudslay's day. Carnegie drawings depicted chronological signs with great accuracy but left other glyphs as impressionistic doodles. Improved drawings appeared only later, with the work of William Coe and Ian Graham. By examining inscriptions at night, when raking light throws eroded features into high relief, Coe and Graham were able to record an extraordinary amount of detail in their scale drawings.

There was a difference in approach, however. Coe focused almost entirely on the texts of Tikal, where he served as project director. Graham's work attempted nothing less than the complete documentation of all monumental inscriptions. This project continues and is likely to last into the next century. It comes none too soon: in the last twenty years the stripping of monuments by looters from unprotected Maya sites has intensified. The looting tends to be inept and often suc-

10   Ian Graham at Yaxchilan, 1975.

ceeds only in destroying inscriptions. Graham's is likely to be the last record of many texts before their disfigurement and theft, as this tragic destruction continues apace.

Glyphs on pottery have also received much attention in the last fifteen years. Michael Coe, brother to William, has published Maya ceramics in 'roll-out' format, a continuous drawing or photographic exposure of a cylindrical surface. Coe proposed that most scenes on ceramics show the Maya 'hero twins', who, according to myth, vanquished death itself in epic underworld struggles. The texts accompanying the twins occur in a rigid sequence, which Coe termed the 'Primary Standard Sequence', 'primary' because of its prominent position on pots and 'standard' because it was so formulaic. It has since been shown that the Primary Standard refers not to myth, as Coe originally thought, but rather to ownership of vessels by particular lords.

Coe's work is part of a larger trend. Increasingly, epigraphers emphasise not only language and history but also the relationship between the highly icono-graphic script and Maya art. At times the line between writing and art is less than clear, as in the elaborate 'full-figure' glyphs, which show signs as dynamic figures, a mass of intertwined limbs, bodies and glyphic elements. It is now the rare epigrapher who ignores the role of art in writing and fails to appreciate the playful quality of this interaction.

With such developments we come uncomfortably close to the present and to the substance of the next chapters. Full decipherment still eludes scholars, but the goal is close with the excellent work of epigraphers such as Victoria Bricker, John Justeson, Floyd Lounsbury, Peter Mathews, Linda Schele and David Stuart. In recent years breakthroughs have come so rapidly that publication has not kept pace. All such progress builds on the lessons of the past. Scholars can no longer afford to ignore information of potential relevance, whether from historical lin-guistics or archaeology, art history or astronomy. Nor can they focus exclusively on one site, one period, one method or one problem, or for that matter regress to inadequate standards of documentation. The complete epigrapher has many skills, but chief among them is the ability to integrate disciplines.

2
Origins, Development and Media

Beginnings

Maya languages are of great age and variety. They originated in the highlands of Guatemala some 4,000 years ago, and split later into thirty-one distinct tongues, some spoken by as many as hundreds of thousands of people, others by only a few hundred. Most are today mutually unintelligible.

Of the greatest importance for decipherment are the subgroups of Yucatecan and Cholan, which occur in the Maya lowlands, a relatively low-lying area to the north and east of the highlands. This region includes parts of Mexico, Guatemala, El Salvador, Honduras and all of Belize. It is where literate Maya civilisation flourished and where the script achieved its most elaborate expression.

11
The Maya region,
with sites mentioned
in the text.

We do not know when the lowlands became Maya speaking. Stone tools indicate human occupation as far back as 9000 BC, and the Maya ceramic tradition is continuous from at least 900 BC onwards. Yet it is impossible to confirm whether the people who used these artefacts spoke Yucatecan or Cholan, likely as that may be. Proof comes only with the advent of literacy at the end of the Preclassic period.

12 Chronology of the Maya region.

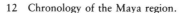

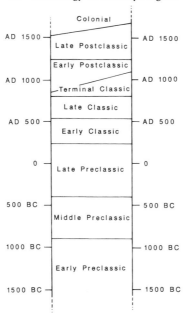

AD 1500	Colonial	AD 1500
	Late Postclassic	
	Early Postclassic	
AD 1000		AD 1000
	Terminal Classic	
	Late Classic	
AD 500		AD 500
	Early Classic	
0	Late Preclassic	0
500 BC		500 BC
	Middle Preclassic	
1000 BC		1000 BC
	Early Preclassic	
1500 BC		1500 BC

Archaeologists customarily divide Maya chronology into several phases. The Preclassic was a time when civilisation developed in a village setting closely tied to the use of agriculture and ceramics. It is further subdivided into 'early', 'middle' and 'late' periods. Only the last two are well documented, embracing the span from about 900 BC to AD 250.

The Preclassic was an era of spectacular accomplishments. Pyramids constructed at the site of El Mirador, in Guatemala, are among the largest structures ever built. They are not merely rehearsals for the architecture of the Classic period (*c.* AD 250 to 900), when Maya writing came into its own, but part of a rich and complex society. Yet it is puzzling that there are so few signs of literacy. Texts that can be linked to the lowlands are generally on portable objects, often from a fairly small area of Belize. Some are on heirlooms from the Olmec civilisation, the first high culture of Mexico and Central America, while others are hewn out of living rock, in caves or on cliff faces. The inscriptions tend to be heavy on pictorial elements, particularly deity heads, and light on linguistic features. The few stelae, or elongated, freestanding stone monuments, have little or no evidence of glyphic inscriptions. One from El Mirador shows many of the elements of later monuments – ruler in frontal pose, ancestral figure floating above – but the composition is cramped and without glyphs.

13
A text on a carved bone from Kichpanha, Belize, 2nd or 3rd century AD.

0

5 cm.

For the origins of writing we must look beyond the lowlands and the highlands to other parts of Central America and Mexico. Specialists know it as 'Mesoamerica', an area stretching from north-central Mexico to Costa Rica. This region, together with the land of the ancient Maya, was culturally unified during pre-Columbian times. It shared a broadly similar calendar, rituals and architecture, although with many differences in detail.

Some time around 700–600 BC parts of the calendar began to be recorded in Mesoamerica, in what is now the Mexican state of Oaxaca. More sophisticated writing, with a calendar based on fixed zero date (the Maya Long Count described in Chapter 1), appeared later in the Isthmus of Tehuantepec and Pacific piedmont of Guatemala. These hieroglyphs date largely from the time of Christ, although there is a little evidence for earlier writing in highland Guatemala. Virtually all are read from top to bottom, in single columns ordered from left to right. Only a handful of texts in the highlands of Guatemala and El Salvador bear signs that are similar to later Maya inscriptions.

The language of the texts is uncertain. For the Isthmus most scholars favour Mixe-Zoquean – a group of related languages – rather than Maya. Mixe-Zoquean is spoken in the area, and some of its words occur in Maya, apparently borrowed at about the time of the first inscriptions in the lowlands.

Thus the background of lowland Maya script is complex and, perhaps in large part, related to other languages. Yet the immediate ancestors were probably in Maya. The few glyphic monuments from the Pacific piedmont of Guatemala and intervening areas – almost certainly areas of Maya speech – depict human figures in ways that became popular in the lowlands. None the less, it may be a mistake to view the origins of writing as a kind of genealogy, with one script begetting another. The cultural unity of Mesoamerica implies a considerable amount of sustained contact, promoting cross-fertilisation that cut across differences of language and culture. Scribal changes probably diffused quite quickly across large areas.

Development and Extinction

Around AD 250 lowland inscriptions began to appear in increasing numbers. From then until AD 900 – the so-called Classic period – writing entered its 'golden age'. Most of the 5,000 or so Maya texts were carved or painted then. As with earlier texts, the focus was entirely on rulers and their retainers. Not for the Maya a mention of the lower classes! And unlike the cuneiform of the Near East, there was not the slightest hint of economic accounts.

The Classic period consisted of four parts. The first is the Early Classic period, lasting from AD 250 to 530, when Maya civilisation crystallised into a new pattern. Artisans fashioned brightly coloured pottery and distinctive architecture with corbelled vaults and 'aprons', a whimsical term for outset moulding. Cities grew both horizontally and vertically as the Maya constructed new buildings upon old. Palaces – suitably rich settings for courtly life – appeared alongside astronomical observatories and burial pyramids. Stelae with altars were dedicated systematically at the end of five-, ten- and twenty-year periods.

The largest site was Tikal, a truly gigantic place many square kilometres in extent. It has the earliest stela with a 'Long Count' – Stela 29. Other cities did not erect monuments until later. Yet Tikal's prominence is often overstated. The site is exceptionally well known, thanks to excavations by the Guatemalan Government and the University of Pennsylvania, and shows every sign of having been culturally precocious and perhaps politically dominant during the first years of the Early Classic period. There were many other villages, towns and cities, however; the story of Tikal is only a partial account of Early Classic civilisation.

14
Historical inscription naming 'Smoking Frog' of Tikal; on Teotihuacan-style ballcourt marker, AD 416.

Early Classic texts can be quite long: some contain over 100 glyphs and leave the impression that most of the writing system was firmly in place. The script also incorporated foreign elements from Teotihuacan, a pre-Columbian metropolis located just north-east of Mexico City. It is unclear whether this influence was imposed by foreign armies or imported by the native élite – the latter is more likely – but end it did, and by about AD 530 Maya civilisation had entered an even more obscure period, the 'hiatus', when the erection of monuments diminished perceptibly in the lowlands, particularly in the north-east corner of Guatemala. This was by no means a uniform phenomenon: a very few sites flourished, while others, such as Tikal, experienced gaps in the historical record a considerable length of time later.

By AD 580 the hiatus was over and the Late Classic period just beginning. Glyphic texts appeared in great quantity and on a wide variety of media, suggesting either widespread literacy or a larger population with the same percentage of readers as before. Certainly there were many people in the lowlands, probably several millions. For the epigrapher the number of texts is sufficient to document nuances of grammar and history that could be only glimpsed before.

Things began to unravel during the Terminal Classic period, starting in about AD 790. Inscriptions showed increasing signs of ineptitude, irregular, almost casual incisions and scant attention to proportion. The contrast with the careful, if stiff, lines of Early Classic texts, and the calligraphic virtuosity of Late Classic inscriptions could hardly be greater. Some monuments have glyphs that are decidedly aberrant, with square outlines, or 'cartouches', of probable non-Maya origin. These changes paralleled the apparent disintegration of Classic society in its heartland around Tikal. Settlement shifted increasingly to lakesides, and the few remaining people built modest buildings with little of the grandeur or ambition of Classic architecture. Other areas, principally northern Yucatan and Belize, were less affected.

We have relatively little writing from the succeeding period, the Postclassic, lasting from about AD 900 to the Spanish Conquest. There are a few stelae, apparently showing deities rather than rulers, some short texts incorporated in murals and, of course, the codices, dating from about AD 1250 to 1450. There seems to have been a marked change in emphasis, with impersonal records replacing true biography, and yet this may be a result of selective preservation. We know from Spanish accounts that native lords kept careful historical records, some possibly copied from glyphs, and that their society continued to show heavy concern for royal lineage and dynastic legitimacy. Perhaps scribes changed their preferred medium from limestone to barkpaper, a material far more vulnerable to decay and Spanish destruction. The last literate Maya probably lived only into the first years of the eighteenth century, just after the conquest of their last major chiefdom in northern Guatemala. Unhappily, their glyphs did not survive them.

Change and Continuity

We do not know for certain whether writing of the fourth century was legible in the fourteenth. Probably it was, despite considerable changes in language and culture; yet, for all its conservatism, there are a number of subtle changes in the script over time.

Some of this is apparent in linguistic structure. Even the earliest texts pay close attention to language, both in word order (subject following verb) and in the pronouns that are so important to understanding phrases in Maya. These are a mere foretaste, however; later inscriptions show greater sophistication, and by the middle of the Early Classic period scribes could record many details of speech.

Phoneticism accounts for much of this flexibility. Early texts include many 'logographs' or word signs, of which a good example might be the picture of a hand for **K'AB**, 'hand' in Yucatec Maya. Phonetic elements help limit the possible range of readings, so that the placement of **ba** after the logograph, or **k'a** just before, would confirm a reading of **K'AB**. Such elements, known as 'phonetic complements', remove much ambiguity. Moreover, the same elements often serve as verbal suffixes, indicating when an event happened and what kind of verb was involved.

The early use of complements and verbal suffixes show that scribes were alive to the sounds of their language and that they had the means to record them. Additional syllables gave fuller expression to written speech. More subtle phrasing, with almost poetical duplication of meaning, became a possibility, and soon fully phonetic spelling found a place alongside logographs. Yet it would be wrong to see these developments in a purely evolutionary sense, a more precise system (phoneticism) gradually replacing an imprecise one (logography). If this were true, Postclassic texts should be entirely phonetic and they are not (though, as with many painted glyphs, they *do* display a decided preference for phonetic spellings). Rather Maya writing continued to be a 'mixed' writing system, combining logographs and phonetic signs.

The script remained highly pictorial for a number of reasons. For one it allowed easy recognition of glyphs without presuming a high degree of literacy. A list of deity names – only rarely spelled phonetically – could be identified without any deep understanding of phoneticism or written grammar. In this way glyphs, especially in monumental inscriptions, remained at least superficially accessible to a larger audience. Codices and other, less public documents were probably more specialised fare.

Another reason was that scribes were much concerned with virtuosity and playful invention. They apparently delighted in giving different versions of the same spelling, using equivalent or near-equivalent signs and alternating logographs with phonetic glyphs. Word signs were an important way to trumpet their learning and skill.

Thus, despite many changes, the script remained essentially conservative. It did not evolve into a completely syllabic system; phoneticism simply made writing more precise, without replacing the rich imagery of pictorial signs.

Regional Variation

Just as early glyphs would be legible in the Postclassic period, so would scribes of Tikal almost certainly understand the inscriptions of Copan. This is not to understate regional differences, however: every area had distinct scribal practices, whether in phrasing or carving technique.

Some sites, particularly Copan and Palenque, contain many inscriptions, with an unusually large inventory of signs. The fuller record suggests an extended circle of literacy, or perhaps deeper knowledge than would be available at small sites erecting only a few monuments. Other cities, particularly in northern Yucatan, recorded dates in an unusual shorthand that is as precise as longer statements and a fraction of the length.

15 An account of stela erection and other events;
basal text of Nim li Punit Stela 2, AD 731.

Among the most marked regionalisms are those from southern Belize, where reading order is obscure and composition strangely compact and irregular. A good example is Stela 2 from Nim li Punit, in southern Belize. Even an experienced eye has difficulty in sorting out phrases.

Another region with a distinct glyphic style is the Puuc, an area of low hills south of the city of Mérida in the Yucatan. With a few exceptions Puuc inscriptions are sufficiently aberrant for epigraphers to have trouble identifying names and segmenting texts into meaningful phrases. The problem is compounded by carving style. Details appear as raised lines on a flat background, and the equal emphasis given outlines and interior forms diminishes legibility considerably. In most other parts of the lowlands glyphs occur as raised blocks. Major outlines are distinguished from decorative incisions by greater width and depth.

Differences in carving are not limited to the Puuc. In some parts of Mexico and Guatemala artisans cut glyphs, not by bevelling edges or cutting at right angles to the stone but by drilling around a block and then undercutting. Such glyphs almost 'float' on the surface, without perceptible connection to the monument. This was probably intended for simple optical effect. Most undercut signs appear on architecture, in panels, stairways and lintels, where inscriptions might be overwhelmed by their monumental setting. Undercutting enhanced legibility by accentuating glyphic outlines.

The most daring carvings, however, are probably those of Copan, which is notable for its full-relief glyphs. It may be no coincidence that trachyte, a relatively soft, easily carved volcanic tuff, was the preferred stone.

Media

The Maya recorded texts by two methods: carving and painting. Both appeared on a wide variety of materials.

Most carvings are of limestone, since, aside from clay and wood, this is by far the most common material in the Maya region. Limestone can range from a dense, almost crystalline stone to a powdery material easily gouged by fingers. A related stone, calcite, which comes from caves, is the finest of these calcium-based stones. Its texture resembles onyx.

Some sites used other stones. The trachyte of Copan comes to mind, but there were also sandstones and slate. The Belizean site of Caracol contains numerous slate monuments, which glisten with mineral inclusions. Unfortunately, a tendency to fracture mars the utility of the stone, and shattered glyphs sometimes occur in the rubble cores of Caracol buildings.

The stone of choice for portable objects was jadeite, or just as often other greenstones, since many pieces are distinct mineralogically from true jade. A hard and uncompromising material, jadeite was sawn, drilled and abraded into finished shape, although glyphs were usually incised. The stone did not lend itself to intricate shapes in high relief.

The technology of carving was fairly crude. Stone was quarried and roughed out with rectangular axes, or in the case of jade carried from distant sources as crudely worked pebbles. More delicate forms emerged after drilling, sawing, chiselling and sanding. The final step was the application of gaudy colours, particularly red, blue, green and yellow. Little of this pigment remains.

Other materials included sapodilla wood (*Manilkara zapota*) – which is noxious to termites and thus useful for lintels and vault beams – conch shells made into trumpets or gorgets, bone, hammered gold (though only during the Postclassic period) and stucco. This last was modelled directly on buildings and often painted blue and red. Occasionally, an idle scribe would scribble glyphs on to the smooth plaster walls of palace and temple rooms. Some such glyphs show great learning and, like the graffiti nearby, preserve a feeling of calligraphic spontaneity that is usually lost in monumental inscriptions.

For the most part surviving inscriptions appear on monuments. The most common was the stela, a rectangular monolith often set into plazas at the centre of Maya cities. Glyphic metaphors indicate that it was perceived as a vegetal object, less the work of humans than nature. In front was an altar, which could be either a simple cylinder or a more elaborate shape, sometimes an animal or deity.

The pairing of stelae and altars has been described as a 'cult'. Doubtless the Maya lavished much attention on them, particularly at the close of key calendrical cycles; but a better way of viewing stelae would be as places for offerings, possibly

16 Fragmentary stela from Caracol, showing offerings dripping
from hand of lord in centre on to low altar at left, c. AD 531.

to ancestors. An image from Caracol apparently illustrates how they were used.
The tree-like stela stands to the left, and in the centre lies an altar on pedestals,
as are indeed found at Caracol. To the right is a ruler pouring liquid, perhaps
blood, upon the altar.

Most other monuments can be viewed in functional terms. Panels set into temple
walls commemorated the dedication of buildings and described whether structures
contained burials, ritual steam-baths or some other feature. Lintels are less easy
to interpret but seem to record events enacted or celebrated in adjoining rooms.
Hieroglyphic stairways served as martial monuments or memorials to ball-playing,
which could be a brutal and bloody sport, sometimes fatal to its participants.

Painting was the other skill of the scribe, and perhaps his earliest medium, since
the ancient word for writing is related to that for 'paint'. The best examples are
the Postclassic codices. Classic art also shows them but as folded sheets bound in
jaguar skin. Alas, none of these survive in legible condition. An even earlier codex
lies in the Mexican National Museum, but present technology cannot separate the
fused pages.

17
Two monkey scribes with codex,
7th or 8th century AD.

All surviving books are written on paper from the inner bark of the fig tree (*Ficus* sp.). The bark was pounded with grooved mallets and shaped into long sheets. After being covered with lime paint, to make the surface smooth, the sheet was folded. The longest screen-fold, the Madrid Codex, is almost seven metres long.

Most known painting is found on more permanent materials. The Classic period has provided a wealth of painted ceramics, many with texts. As Michael Coe has pointed out, the designs on one group of looted pots from northern Guatemala even resemble codices. The palette includes red for the edges of sheets, black for details and cream for neutral background. Lines have a 'whiplash' quality, as if snapped suddenly for maximum calligraphic effect. Coe described the pots as 'codex-style', the work of scribes who also decorated codices. None the less, the texts refer to ceramics and cannot have been copied directly from books.

18
Scene from codex-style vessel,
with spirit companion of a Maya ruler,
7th or 8th century AD.

The greatest extant achievement of the calligrapher was a set of three painted rooms at the ruins of Bonampak in Chiapas, Mexico. Other murals are known from Belize, Guatemala and northern Yucatan, as in a Postclassic painting from Coba; and there are also extraordinary cave paintings from the site of Naj Tunich, in Guatemala. But they cannot match Bonampak's composition, brilliant range of colours and integration of detail with overall design.

The rooms display scenes that envelop the viewer, who becomes immersed in historical events of 1,000 years ago. The first room celebrates the designation of an heir to the throne, who is presented to a gathering of lords in court uniform. As in all rooms, glyphic captions explain the event and identify people. Dancers in quetzal feather robes enliven the event by moving to the accompaniment of musicians dressed as supernaturals. The second room commemorates a war or, rather, a bloody mêlée intended primarily to capture sacrificial victims. The same room shows the resulting carnage: a beheaded victim, the laceration of finger tips and captives gazing up in mute appeal. Glyphic texts identify the victor as Yahaw Chan Muwan, Lord of Bonampak. The final room, which was never finished, shows equally bloody activities, with more sacrifice and blood-letting, this time by members of the court. Unfortunately, few glyphs can be read here.

19 Wall painting from the Las Pinturas temple at Coba;
refers to various gods (*top row*) and the offerings to them (*second and third rows*),
including fish, venison, maize cakes and human hearts, *c.* AD 1300.

20
Painted glyphs on cave wall,
Naj Tunich, Guatemala,
c. AD 741.

In a number of places we glimpse texts painted or woven on representations of textiles. These are also documented on a few monuments, usually on hems. Presumably many texts, perhaps even a majority, were once on perishable objects.

21
Yahaw Chan Muwan of Bonampak,
from Room 2 of the Bonampak murals,
c. AD 792.

Who were the Scribes?

David Stuart has recently shown that Classic scribes were anything but anony-
mous. In about a dozen examples they left their names after the expression *u tz'ib*,
'his painting'. Of these only one name is repeated twice: it appears on two vessels
displaying an obese lord who probably commissioned the pots.

It is likely that scribes were of fairly high status, with large residences, as have
recently been discovered at Copan. One pot tells us that the artist was a member
of the royal family of Naranjo, Guatemala. Others reveal possible patron gods of
monkey-like appearance, including one who sprouts what seems to be computer
print-out! Yet scribal signatures are relatively rare, and Mayanists will probably
never match the detailed information on Classical Greek painters.

In contrast, about seventy signatures appear on sculpture. They are a little perplexing, however. Pots always have a single scribe; stelae record as many as eight.
Did the sculptors work consecutively? Or was there a tangle of elbows as artists
finished different parts of the monument? We shall probably never know, although
the practice of employing many artists is not entirely surprising. A sculpture
represents a vast undertaking made more rapid by a large workforce.

The status of sculptors is less clear than that of painters. At the least, sculptors
may have enjoyed some mobility. Monuments at capitals and subordinate sites are
occasionally by the same hand, although, of course, these could simply have been

dragged from a central workshop; the fact that many were relatively small suggests as much. Yet there are also hints that rulers did not wish to give too much attention to their artists or overvalue their skill. Some sites, such as Dos Pilas and Tikal, are remarkable for the absence of signatures, while neighbouring sites have many. Perhaps sculptors did not all enjoy the same position in society, or at least their rulers entertained different ideas of what was suitable for public display.

22   Sculptor's signature on Arroyo de Piedra Stela 1, *c.* AD 611.

3
Structure of Mayan Writing

Spelling

Glyphic spelling is a complex matter, with what seem to be contradictory rules and confused categories of signs; yet there is order in this apparent chaos.

The basic unit is the glyph, an irreducible sign with a distinct meaning or sound. Virtually all have slightly rounded edges, although there is a tremendous variety of form. Some appear as elaborate, almost baroque shapes, others as crude sketches with little more than essential details. To impose some order on this variety epigraphers distinguish between 'main signs', or relatively large, rounded signs, and the smaller, elongated 'affixes' that cluster around them. However, this distinction meant little to the Maya, who freely alternated the two.

The next highest unit is the 'compound', which resembles nothing less than a group of balloons – in this case distinct glyphs – wedged tightly against one another.

The significance of the compound is not entirely clear. It helps segment a text into neat blocks, but perhaps as much for spacing as any other reason. The same signs were just as easily spread over several compounds.

Reading order within a compound is consistent but by no means rigid. The affixes to the left or top – known as 'prefixes' – were read first. Those to the bottom and right – the 'postfixes' – came last. The centre, a place usually occupied by a main sign, was read in between. This diagram gives an idea of the sequence:

2

1   3   5

4

It is here that we get our first glimmering of reading order: let to right and top to bottom. There are also a few exceptions, however. The **AHAW** title, which refers to the very highest office of the Classic Maya, often occurs as a prefix, or more precisely a 'superfix', since it appears on top of other signs (position 2 in the diagram). By rights it should be read before the glyph positions 3, 4 and 5; yet it is instead the final sign in the spelling, and sometimes appears as such, in a variant, main sign form.

David Stuart has shown that another superfix, apparently representing maize foliage, functions in the same way. The example illustrated here should be **yi-NAL-chi** but in fact reads **yi-chi-NAL**, or *yichnal*, 'together with' in Cholan. The compound separates the name glyphs of Maya lords and tells us that they did something together, the second person supervising the first.

(subordinate) + *yichnal* + (superordinate)

Scribes had other tricks as well. Rather than string out a long series of glyphs, in an arrangement tedious to both reader and carver, they combined or 'conflated' signs into a single form, with the distinctive markings of one glyph placed in, or next to, another. This saved space (always a consideration on a small monument), yet also left enough details for easy reading. Similarly, scribes overlapped signs, so that only one side showed, or 'infixed' glyphs entirely, with one encased in a second. These spellings are complex but, given a proper understanding of the rules, quite legible.

Types of signs

Affixes, main signs and compounds are defined by size and shape. A second and more interesting approach is to define signs by function. Consider a symbol that most people see upon entering a non-smoking room:

It does not especially resemble anything (aside from the smoking cigarette), yet we know it to mean 'smoking not permitted here'. This is an 'ideograph', a sign communicating an idea. In Chapter 2 we were introduced to other kinds of signs, including 'logographs' and 'complements'. All have a role in Maya script.

The best example of an ideograph is probably the cartouche that encloses day signs. For unknown reasons some early examples have a slight similarity to the *Spondylus* shell, which served during the Classic period as a scoop for blood.

There is little indication that the cartouche corresponded to a particular word, although its meaning as a container of day signs must have been clear enough.

The problem with ideographs is that they might well have been associated with words. Available evidence simply fails to prove it. In this sense ideographs form a default category about which we know relatively little.

Logographs are much better understood. By far the most common are the numbers. Before looking at them, however, we need to understand recent Maya numeration, which provides a useful baseline.

Numbers

Our numbering is decimal, based on the number ten or its multiples. The Maya system is vigesimal and emphasises twenty and it multiples. Numbers in between are filled by unique numerals up to ten, followed by combinations of ten with numbers between one and nine. 'Thirteen', for example, is *oxlahun*, or '3 + 10'. This is not too far different from our own system.

The similarity may have something to do with the origins of Maya counting. Many peoples count by tallies on the hand, so that words for 'five' and 'ten' refer to the completion of one hand, then two. Despite their vigesimal system, the Maya number in the same way. The word for 'ten' in Yucatec Maya, *lahun*, may derive from a root for 'end, finish, complete', and the word for twenty is the same as that for 'man' in some highland languages. The allusion is clearly to the full number of fingers and toes.

Higher numbers can be expressed in two ways. One method anticipates the completion of the next higher unit, as in *kan tu yox k'al*, 'four in the third score', for forty-four. The expression both anticipates the completion of the third twenty-year period (60) and indicates the number (4) within that period. The second method is more like our own. It uses a conjunction to combine the number of twenty-year periods with a smaller number. Accordingly, forty-four could also be *ka k'al katak kan*, 'two-twenty and four'. By using this system with additional multiples of twenty the Maya can count into hundreds of thousands and beyond.

Numbers as logographs

The glyphic system is slightly different. Dots record the numbers one to four, and bars stand for units of five. Fourteen, then, is represented by four dots and two bars (4 + 5 + 5 = 14).

Except in rare cases of reversed reading order, the dots *always* appear to the left or on top of bars. It is interesting that the number one was sometimes rendered as a single finger, perhaps recalling tallies done on the hand.

The origin of this system is almost certainly non-Maya. The dots may register counts of pebbles or cacao beans (a valuable commodity in Mesoamerica) and make their first appearance in the Mexican state of Oaxaca. The bars are documented in the Isthmus of Tehuantepec well before their introduction to the Maya lowlands.

Occasionally, 'head variants' – pictorial signs in the shape of human, animal or deity heads – alternate with numbers. These are still somewhat perplexing. The variant for *bolon*, 'nine', which depicts the head of supernatural youth, is read elsewhere as *yax*, even though *bolon* is the likely reading in tabulations. Similarly, the variant for *lahun*, 'ten', a human skull, does not have the same reading in other contexts.

BOLON   **LAHUN**

Scribes met the challenge of writing ordinal numbers in an expression elucidated by Linda Schele. 'Second', for example, was transcribed by using the cardinal number *ka* in the phrase **u-ka-?-l(a)**, 'his two?' The middle glyph is undeciphered.

'his second katun as lord'

Large numbers fascinated the ancient Maya, who recorded them in more efficient and ambitious ways than their descendants. One example is that for recording numbers between twenty and thirty-nine. Scribes replaced four bars with the so-called 'moon sign', **K'AL**, and then added the requisite number of bars and dots, so that thirty-one would consist of **K'AL** preceded by two bars and one dot.

An expression closer to that of modern Yucatec (as in *kan tu yox k'al*) is found only in the Dresden Codex.

Even larger numbers are found only in connection with the calendar, which is discussed later in this chapter (see p. 48).

Before leaving this topic we should emphasise that there was also the concept of 'vacancy' – 'zero' or 'null' if you will, although some believe the notion might have been closer to 'completion of cycle'. In Postclassic times this was represented by a shell. Earlier examples show an element with three lobes. These glyphs are of fundamental importance to the Maya place notation system, described with the calendar (see p. 49).

Logographs and rebus

Maya script shows a keen sensitivity to homophones – words of similar sound but different meaning. Such words, or rather the signs for them, were used interchangeably in a playful rebus.

Two examples come to mind. The first is an affix often used as a locative preposition (such as 'in' or 'at' in English). It appears in a bewildering range of shapes: torches, bundles of sticks (usually smoking), wooden poles, a vulture head and others. The Maya treated them as equivalent signs, doubtless because the words for these objects were similar or identical to *ta*, the locative preposition in Cholan. The vulture was identified in Chol as *taʔ-hol*, 'excrescence head', and the terms for pine and torch were *taaj*.

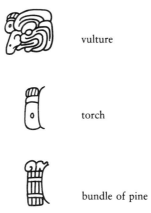

vulture

torch

bundle of pine

The second example owes its existence to equally close homophones, in this case the words for 'snake', 'sky' and the number 'four'.

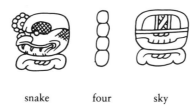

| snake | four | sky |

In most Maya languages these differ only in the length of the vowel, a feature scribes frequently (if not always) ignored. Where the number is called for, 'snake' or 'sky' may appear. And where 'sky', 'snake'. The homophones even make their way into Maya art. Celestial or sky bands have snake-like skin or are replaced by intertwined serpents. Probably these are homophonic witticisms.

Syllabic spelling

Another kind of sign is the phonetic syllable. As Knorosov showed, it is a consonant/vowel combination that joins with other syllables to make words. **Wi** + **tzi** or *witz*, 'hill', is one such spelling. It sometimes alternates, in well-controlled contexts, with a logograph showing stone markings, and seems to have been not only a term for hills but a metaphor for some stelae and pyramids. It is probably no coincidence that the Classic Maya buried their rulers in artificial 'hills', and that modern Maya venerate real mountains as the seats of ancestral spirits.

The important point to make is that phonetic spellings bear no relation to the origin of the phonetic sign. **Lu** probably derives from the picture of a catfish, *lu?*; **k'u** from the image of a bird nest, *k'u?*; **ka** from a general word for fish, *kay*; **na** from the head of a woman or mother, *na?*, and so on. Yet these meanings are irrelevant to syllabic spellings. This is what made phoneticism so controversial: it suggested that the Maya used elements smaller than a morpheme, the smallest unit of meaning.

Ironically, although Thompson opposed phoneticism, his discoveries led to its eventual acceptance. Thompson had argued that one sign, **te**, 'tree', could also appear in places where it had a very different sense.

Cases in point were the so-called 'numerical classifiers', terms inserted between numbers and the things thus numbered. Classifiers are obligatory in speech and specify the qualities of the item being quantified: whether something is heaped, laid in a row, or whether it is long, small, heavy, human, plant or animal. Although some languages have many classifiers, a few general ones, such as *te*, apply to most kinds of object. These are the ones recorded in script.

By proving that a logograph for 'tree' could be used as a classifier, Thompson established that sounds had to be distinguished from function. It was no longer useful to talk about numerical classifier glyphs, only about glyphs that could also be numerical classifiers. The distinction may seem fine but it is quite important and, to some degree, still goes unheeded, particularly by those who speak of 'verbal affixes' and the like. Thompson had pointed the way to a phonetic approach by concentrating on the sounds rather than the meaning of signs. It was only a short step to recognising that those sounds could be combined or used singly.

Another of Knorosov's theories was that phonetic spellings were 'synharmonic', that is, the vowel of the second syllable corresponded to the first. On the whole he seems to have been right. Even though the Maya usually dropped the final, 'dead' vowel, they tended to match the vowels. In this the writing strongly resembles some syllabic scripts of the eastern Mediterranean; but there are many exceptions, including two spellings for a glyph meaning 'drill' – ho-ch'(o) or ho-ch'(a). In either case the reading was *hoch'*.

ho-ch'(o)   ho-ch'(a)

Thanks to recent decipherments, the spelling rules of phoneticism are coming into focus. It is now clear that syllables simply provide a collection of sounds; they do not tell us how those sounds are broken down morphemically. As an example, consider the spelling of the verb 'see' or perhaps 'witness'. It may be rendered in many ways and in various groupings of logographs and syllables:

yi-IL-ah (syll.-log.-syll)   **yi-la-h(i)** (syll.-syll.-syll.)   **yi-l(i)-a-h(i)** (syll.-syll.-syll.-syll.)

These illustrate the complexity of spellings which, depending on the whim of the scribe, range from purely phonetic groupings to mixtures of syllables and a logograph – here a human eye with lines coming out, read IL. In morphemic terms, however, all can be broken down into a possessive pronoun *u* (shifting to *y* before vowels), a root *il*, 'see', and a suffix denoting both verbal inflection and 'tense'. The reader is thus obliged to process the spelling into grammatically meaningful units, which are not expressed explicitly in writing.

Another spelling rule takes this even further. As we have seen, the crucial distinction is between transcription – a true reflection of signs – and transliteration –

how these signs spell words or phrases that make sense. In some instances the Maya provided a spelling that was incomplete. If read literally, it would be difficult to understand; but if the reader added key elements, it could be transliterated into meaningful Maya.

This can hardly be said to be a common feature of the script, yet it is present in a few examples. One is the turtle head *a*, sometimes represented by a beak only. In several contexts it supplies an *a*, as in the spelling of the month sign **K'AN-a-si-y(a)**, *k'anasi*.

K'AN
a
si
y(a)

. . . or in a spelling for 'turtle',

a-k(u), *ak*

which is interchangeable with a logograph . . .

AK

But it also occurs as a 'proclitic' – a morpheme without accent that is prefixed to a word. Here it should read *ah* but does not: presented with an *a*, the reader had to add an *h* to yield a proclitic. Such omissions, usually of consonants, seem to have occurred especially in spellings with two or more syllables, as in the glyphs for *tz'unun*, 'hummingbird':

tz'u-nu

This, too, is highly similar to ancient Mediterranean scripts such as Linear B, which records *Knossos* – the city – as **ko-no-so**.

We now know of about 100 phonetic elements, including variants. As shown by gaps in the syllablic chart, this is probably only about half of those the Maya used. Consonant + *e* and consonant + *o* combinations in particular are poorly documented. A large number doubtless await discovery.

23 Portion of syllabic chart.

Yet the chart also shows that many signs have the same reading. No fewer than twelve glyphs record the vowel *u*; there are at least four **na**, four **pa**, three **ba** and three **ka**. In part this embarrassment of signs results from the long development of the script, which gained new ways to render a sound and kept some old. Scribal skill and pride of craft probably encouraged this trend. The more signs in the scribe's bag of tricks, the greater the variety, the less the visual tedium of repeated glyphs.

There is one feature that is not apparent in the chart. This is 'polyvalency' – the existence of signs with many different readings. In syllables it cannot have played a large role, although this is less true for other kinds of glyphs. The logograph **KAWAK**, for example, was also read **TUN** or syllabic **ku**.

syllable **ku**   logograph **TUN**   logograph **KAWAK**

Both context and complements help narrow the reading to the appropriate choice.

Grammar

With syllables epigraphers have a powerful tool for studying glyphic grammar. Phonetic spelling, if not always an exact record of speech, at least provides something close to it: an approximation of the sounds and grammatical particles of languages spoken up to 1,800 years ago. It is for this reason that glyphs are so exciting to linguists. Students of Romance languages take for granted the existence of written precursors like Latin – a neat check on inferences about linguistic development; but here, for the first time in pre-Columbian studies, we have the same for a native American language. Hypothetical reconstructions may now be compared with fairly accurate, if selective, records of Preclassic, Classic and Postclassic speech.

We are fortunate to have a good knowledge of modern Maya languages, on which all reconstructions are based. The most relevant are the Yucatecan and Cholan subgroups, which occur (or did so until the seventeenth century) in the areas where there are inscriptions. There is little doubt that the languages of the texts represent earlier or related forms of them.

The evidence for this is varied. Sound shifts found only in Cholan are attested in inscriptions, as are distinctive positional suffixes. (In fact, a seventeenth-century document in Chontal – a Cholan tongue – reads astonishingly like a transcription from Classic texts.) In other texts specific idioms and locational prepositions implicate Yucatecan. Tzeltalan, a close cousin to Cholan, contributes very few words.

Yucatecan and Cholan make free use of certain sounds, with five vowels (six in Chol) and nineteen consonants. Some of the latter are 'glottalised' (as in *k'*, *ch'* and *tz'*), produced by sudden constrictions of the larynx after the articulation of the consonant. The effect is guttural and somewhat foreign to the ear of English speakers.

Vowels and consonants combine to produce the roots of words, which are fairly predictable in structure: a consonant, a vowel and another consonant. Yucatec is unusual among Mayan languages in that it is also tonal – that is, changes in vowel pitch denote differences in meaning. This feature is more common in other parts of Mesoamerica.

In English word order is subject-verb-object, as in 'I ate the tortilla'. Quite a different sequence awaits us in Yucatecan and Cholan, where conventional order is verb-subject in intransitive phrases and verb-object-subject in transitive.

Of the highest importance in this scheme are inflections that appear before or after Maya roots. Nouns, for example, are inflected for possession. Thus the Yucatec expression *y-ahaw-il*, 'his lord', consists of three parts: a noun (*ahaw* or 'lord'), a possessive pronoun (*y-* or 'his, hers, its') and a noun suffix (*-il*). The suffix appears to be optional in some languages.

Similarly, verbs are inflected for number (singularity or plurality) and person (first, second or third). Transitive verbs require that inflections agree with subject and object.

The basic element in inflections is the pronoun. Linguists divide these into two sets: the 'ergative', which indicates the person of the subject of a transitive verb, and the 'absolutive', which expresses the direct object of transitive verbs and the subject of intransitives. The ergative is also used for possession (as in the *y-* in *y-ahaw-il*). All pronouns in this set are prefixes, while the absolutive consists of suffixes.

An interesting twist to this 'ergative' structure (as it is labelled by linguists) is that it is not always applied consistently. In references to past events Cholan intransitive verbs use the absolutive set for subject agreement. This is, of course, fully compatible with an ergative system. In references to the present, however, the same verbs use the *ergative* set for subject agreement.

Compare the two phrases *woli k-och-el*, 'I am entering', with *tzaʔ och-iy-on*, 'I entered'. In the first example *k-* is the ergative pronoun 'I'. In the second, a past event, the pronoun is *-on*, of the absolutive set. This inconsistency is described as 'split ergativity' because it does not appear in every context but only in selected tenses.

Tenses are also marked by suffixes and, optionally, by prefixes. These elements allow speakers of Maya to express events in the present and past, as well as actions that are imperative, conditional, remote or unlikely. Some verbs have suffixes that encode for position, such as whether someone is sitting or lying down; numerical classifiers reflect similar concepts.

Glyphic grammar

Parts of Maya languages are beginning to be documented in glyphs. Some of this is not quite new: the ergative pronoun *u* was recognised at an early date from Bishop Landa's syllabary. Nor can we state that there is complete unanimity among linguists about glyphic grammar, but progress is fast now, and we can hazard a few general statements.

Word order is clearly very similar. Whorf suggested as much in the 1930s, but it was Proskouriakoff who confirmed it through her discovery of grammatical subjects in Classic inscriptions. A useful illustration is:

Transcription: **chu-ka-h(a)/?/u-ba-k(i)/ ya-?-BALAM**

Transliteration: *Chuk-ah ? u bak ya-x-balam*

Translation: 'Was captured ?, the captive of "Bird Jaguar"'

The verb comes first – a suffixed element marks verbal inflection – and is followed by the name of the captive (whose ultimate fate was doubtless grim).

Such word order may be complicated by the insertion of prepositional phrases between verb and subject:

Transcription: **CHUM-wa-ni/ta-AHAW-le-l(e)/ya-AHAW-te K'INICH**

Transliteration: *Chum-wan-i ta ahaw-lel y-ahaw-te k'in-ich*

Translation: 'Was seated in the lordship, *Yahawte k'inich*'

Note the many affixes written with phonetic syllables. The verb root is *chum*, 'sit', followed by the suffix *wan-i*, to indicate inflection for verbs having to do with position. Next comes the prepositional phrase, which ends with the name of the lord who acceded to the throne.

Ergative pronouns, here in the transitive, also make an appearance:

Transcription: **u-?-wa/ch'a-h(i) 'Ruler 2'**

Transliteration: *u-?-wa ch'ah* 'Ruler 2'

Translation: 'he scatters (?) the droplets, "Ruler 2"'

This phrase differs slightly from the first two. It has an ergative pronoun (*u*) and a transitive suffix for the present tense (*wa*). The direct object is *ch'ah*, 'droplets', which are scattered by the logograph of a human hand.

More rarely the Maya recorded events in the future. One common verb, *ut*, meaning 'happen, come to pass, to be done', usually appears in the past tense:

Transcription: **u-ti-y(a)**

Transliteration: *ut-i*

Translation: 'it happened'

In a few examples, however, it is also attested in the future.

Transcription: **u-to-m(a)**

Transliteration: *ut-om*

Translation: 'it will happen'

Another instance is a glyph meaning 'end', *lah*, often spelled with a mixture of logograph and syllables. The more usual form is in the past tense.

Transcription: **LAH-y(i)**

Transliteration: *lah-i*

Translation: 'was completed'

However, in a text at the Mexican site of Tortuguero the verb root *lah* appears with the future suffix -*om*.

Transcription: **LAH-ho-m(a)**

Transliteration: *lah-om*

Translation: 'will be completed'

The preceding event is the dedication of the structure containing the text, and very likely the scribe was relating the temple dedication to the completion of an important calendrical cycle some years in the future.

Noun suffixes also appear in glyphs. Take, for example, the title

Transcription: **a-na-b(i)**

Transliteration: *anab*

Translation: not known

This occurs in variant spellings inflected for possession:

Transcription: **ya-a-na-bi-l(i)**

Transliteration: *y-anab-il* (-*il* is the noun suffix)

Translation: 'his *anab*'

The one feature in which the script is limited is in its supreme impersonality. On present evidence all known texts are in the third person singular, with suggestions here and there of 'split ergativity'. There are no plural forms, no autobiographical boasts, no exhortations or imperatives. Apparently we have received only the phrasing of the scribes, who by their indirect language perhaps enhanced the solemnity of Maya historical records.

Glyphic phrasing

Glyphic sentences are usually embedded in long texts. The standard method for recording them is in linear sequences of compounds or, far more frequently, in rows and columns of signs. By modern convention rows are transcribed with numbers, the columns with letters. A compound can thus be said to occupy position B2 – in the second row and second column. The reading order in compounds (left to right, top to bottom) can also be observed in texts but in double columns. Here by reading order:

$$1 \quad 2 \quad 7 \quad 8 \quad 13$$

$$3 \quad 4 \quad 9 \quad 10 \quad 14$$

$$5 \quad 6 \quad 11 \quad 12 \quad 15$$

24 Dos Pilas Stela 15, AD 721.

Odd columns are read singly from top to bottom, as above. Aberrant reading order (retrograde, or right to left) is exceedingly unusual and may have been determined largely by non-glyphic considerations, such as the architectural placement of a particular monument.

Texts can be divided into 'clauses', which usually have the same structure: a chronological statement, helping to place an event in time, followed by the verb and subject. The subjects tend to consist of accession names (often inherited from some ancestor, sometimes a grandfather) and a long string of titles that announce the authority and puissance of the lord. In a few inscriptions, such as a stela from Dos Pilas, there are multiple clauses connected with a single day.

Floyd Lounsbury has documented one glyphic feature that is relatively common in modern Maya discourse. This is the couplet, a set of two or more parallel clauses, occasionally with ellipsis or omission of the subject. The clauses record related ideas. The images thus conjured form almost a poetic cascade of alternative phrasings and supplementary information.

The Calendar

The Maya felt a strong need to fix events in time and to segment their texts into clauses introduced by dates. For this they devised an elaborate calendar, the most complex in Mesoamerica. Parts of it were probably non-Maya in origin and originated, we can be sure, for practical reasons (a farmer's almanac) or for more esoteric ones (divination and augury). Even at an early date the latter were probably far more important. Historic evidence suggests that an individual's date of birth became part of his name, with an effect on personality and fate. Maya rulers of the Classic period do not seem to have followed this practice.

The Maya calendar consists of cycles of short and long duration. Each eventually pivots, much like a cog in clockwork, to its starting position. Within this system a day has a unique position: on cog-wheel A it is in a certain place, on cog-wheel B in another, and so on. No other day shares precisely the same combination of calendrical positions.

To the Maya time had a linear aspect, a stately progression of days, but of even greater importance was the repetition of cycles. In this way an event in remote antiquity, perhaps presided over by gods, might be linked with a contemporary action, since both were associated with similar places in Maya cycles. In the Postclassic and Colonial periods this perception of time formed the basis of twenty-year prophecies.

The first cycle in Maya glyphs is the 'Sacred Round', also known by the ersatz term 'Tzolkin'. It is a period of 260 days composed of combinations of the numbers one to thirteen and twenty day names. After 260 days the cycle begins again (13 × 20 = 260). Our names for the day signs are taken from the indispensable 'Account' by Bishop Landa.

The next cycle is the 'Haab', or 'Vague Year' – 'vague' because it lasts 365 days, just shy of a solar year, yet sufficiently discrepant to stray quickly from the tropical year. It contains eighteen months, each twenty days long, and a period of five days at the end of the cycle.

The Haab joins with the Sacred Round to form yet another period: one of 18,980 days or fifty-two years. This goes by the name 'Calendar Round' and is the most common unit for recording dates in the inscriptions, as in the example '4 Cauac 12 Zip', which will not recur for a complete Calendar Round. To peoples of Central Mexico the end of this cycle represented nothing less than an existential crisis: the world would disintegrate if priests failed to kindle special fires in the breasts of sacrificial victims. Houses were swept of debris, objects of value destroyed and buried. In only one part of the Classic Maya area – a ritual rubbish pit in the province of Chiapas, Mexico – is there the slightest evidence for this rite.

In addition to the Calendar Round there are cycles of nine days and 819 days. The first apparently refers to sequences of gods, the second perhaps to rituals associated with the erection of effigies in different parts of Classic-period sites. The colour symbolism so pervasive in Mesoamerica formed a key part of this ritual.

Larger counts of days were recorded by means of a place notation system, known as the Long Count. We transcribe it from right to left, in increasingly higher units separated by dots. The units are

> 144,000 days or *baktun* (or 20 *katun*)
> + 7,200 days or *katun* (or 20 *tun*)
> + 360 days or *tun* (or 18 *uinal*)
> + 20 days or *uinal* (or 20 *kin*)
> + 1 day or *kin*

so that 9.8.12.12.8, or 9 *baktun*, 8 *katun*, 12 *tun*, 12 *uinal* and 8 *kin*, total 1,358,168 days.

The crucial unit is the *tun*, a word for both a period of 360 days and 'stone'. Almost certainly the latter reflects the ancient custom of erecting stone monuments at the end of some calendrical phases. However, there are indications that the names for periods differed slightly during the Classic period and varied from site to site. *Kin* and *uinal* (or *uinik*) are documented, but the term for units for 360 days may also have been **HAAB**, and that for 7,200 days **WINAL** (or **WINIK**) **HAAB**. Even higher units are known, including one of $142 \ 10^{30}$ years! Our universe is considerably younger than this span.

But from what were these place notations counted? The base date lay in the distant past, in 3114 BC. Given what we know of the Maya, who were not yet settled in villages, 3114 BC must be a retroactive date, perhaps devised around the time of Christ.

Another term for the Long Count is the Initial Series, because it often appears first in inscriptions. Subsequent dates are counted backwards and forwards from this chronological anchor by means of Distance Numbers: ordered lists of *kin*, *uinal*, *tun*, etc. Indeed, from various clues it is clear that the Initial Series itself was regarded as a Distance Number from its base date. The Distance Number specifies precisely the difference in time between Calendar Round notations and provides a useful way of linking them to larger cycles.

25   Arroyo de Piedra Stela 3, with Initial Series text, AD 731.

One sometimes hears that such counts were 'more accurate' than other systems. Nonsense: the calendar reckoned by whole days and as such could not deal easily with fractional sums, which would be necessary for accurate estimates of some planetary and lunar phenomena. The only hint of shorter reckonings are the so-called 'Puuc-style' dates, where the numeral of the month is one less than expected. A few scholars feel that these express night-time events, after the beginning of a new day in the Sacred Round but before the start of a new day in the Vague Year. This arrangement presumes that the cycles did not start at the same hour.

The correlation problem

The obvious challenge in working with Long Count dates is determining the relationship with the European calendar. The Maya at the time of Spanish contact left some ambiguous references to equivalences between their day count and ours but always in reference to cycles smaller than the Long Count, which had lapsed into desuetude some centuries before. This has caused much grief to archaeologists, who need a reliable correlation to date their finds.

The majority of specialists now favour a correlation proposed by Goodman (1905), and refined by the Mexican scholar Juan Martínez Hernández and Eric Thompson (both 1927), with subsequent modifications by Floyd Lounsbury (1982). This would place, for example, the long Count 9.15.10.0.0 at 30 June AD 741, exactly 1,407,600 days after the beginning of the Long Count on 13 August 3114 BC. Radiocarbon dates from carved lintels and astronomical data, particularly accounts of warfare invoking the planet Venus, lend strong support to this correlation. Still unresolved are some perplexing disparities in the archaeology of Yucatan, which suggest a 'short' chronology and a greatly compressed Postclassic period.

4
Glyphs as History

The decipherments of Berlin and Proskouriakoff revolutionised Maya studies by showing that glyphs from the Classic period recorded the names and deeds of native lords. Epigraphers have since revealed much more, including accounts of courtly officials, warriors, scribes and sculptors, ladies of the blood and sacrificial captives. From this, history is being written, although it is of a very special sort: the texts present the concerns of the élite only, in documents doubtless edited for content.

Classic Royalty

At the core of Classic society was a small group of hereditary lords whose parentage was of consuming interest. Many dozens of 'parentage statements' – really a set of titles in father/mother pairs – spell out precisely who fathered or mothered whom. The most common are:

Translation: 'his child (of man)' or 'X's child'

(a)

(b, a variant)

Transcription: **ya-l(a)**

Transliteration: *y-al*

Translation: 'her child (of woman)' or 'Y's child'

The structure of the texts leaves little doubt about their meaning, although only a few are completely deciphered. Much like our own expressions for kinship (such as 'blood kin'), some are metaphors for 'blood' or 'blood-letting'.

In addition, there are several references to siblings, as in:

Transcription: **yi-tz'i- n(i)**

Transliteration: *y-itz'in*

Translation: *'his younger brother'*

Other terms will probably be found, and the prospects are good for reconstructing accurate genealogies. The glyphs have already been useful in confirming the patrilineal basis for royal descent and in showing that the 'crown' could pass from brother to brother before descending to the next generation.

Through a phrase meaning 'succession' or 'change' the Maya specified the position of a ruler in a dynastic sequence:

Transcription: **u-5 + 20/'HEL'/? 'founder'**

Rough translation: 'its twenty-fifth succession since the dynastic founder'

This is a count of rulers extending back to the real or mythological founders of dynasties, whose names sometimes follow. It is not unusual to find counts of twenty-five or thirty rulers, yet neither are these common. Many sites, including several important ones, avoided lists altogether. Perhaps their dynasties were of more recent origin, or had an interrupted succession of rulers. In such cases we presume the lords did not want to draw attention to a shallow dynastic genealogy or an insecure claim to the throne.

Rulers did not lack for titles. Occasionally they boasted of the number of captives taken in battle:

Transcription: **ah-HUN-K'AL-ba-k(i)**

Transliteration: *ah hun k'al bak*

Translation: 'he of the twenty-one captives'

For such warlike people twenty-one captives hardly seem worth mentioning, yet perhaps 'twenty-one' meant 'more than twenty'; or conceivably a low count of captives referred to the number of *high-status* prisoners. The matter is still unresolved.

The most important title, however, was that of *ahaw*, 'lord', which appears in a bewildering variety of forms:

Only a few members of each generation used this title, and all were immediate members of the royal family. The Bonampak murals – arguably the greatest pre-Columbian paintings yet found – show that royal heirs became *ahawob* (plural of *ahaw*) in rites of dazzling splendour: the nobility acclaimed the heir to the accompaniment of dancing and music, and then set forth to capture sacrificial victims.

Ahaw is most common in the 'Emblem glyph' identified by Heinrich Berlin. Berlin preferred not to place too precise a meaning on the sign, yet he did show that the main signs within the Emblem varied from site to site. Presumably they named a town or ruling dynasty.

More recent studies indicate that the main sign is in fact a 'toponym' or place name. Thus a lord might be the *ahaw* of the **K'AN WITZ NAL**, 'yellow hill.'

Transcription: **? K'AN-WITZ-NAL / AHAW**

Transliteration: **? K'an Witznal Ahaw**

Translation: '? Yellow Hill Lord'

Such place names are quite common in the texts and generally refer to geographical landmarks, such as bodies of water or prominent hills.

Some scholars go further. From distributional evidence they argue that Emblems represent 'polity names', glyphs that proclaim lordship over territory rather than places. Toponyms provide some support for this interpretation.

Tikal   Copan   Yaxchilan   Arroyo de Piedra

26 Important Emblem glyphs from the Late Classic period.

Emblems are at first rare. Only later, towards the end of the Early Classic, do they appear with the initial sign, and it is at that point that place names occur both in Emblems and *separately*, as distinct 'toponymic statements' at the end of a text. That is, in the beginning the Maya did not find it necessary to distinguish between Emblems and place names – after all, rulership probably extended only over fairly small areas with one or two settlements. To be *ahaw* of a place was, by definition, to be *ahaw* of a polity. Only later, when sites grew and dynasties came to rule several centres, did scribes find it useful to distinguish between the more general concept – 'lord of such-and-such a kingdom', as embodied in the Emblem – and 'such-and-such a place', as found in toponymic statements. Most likely the main sign of the Emblem derived from the location of the first palace and temples, the heart of the polity and the principal seat of the dynasty.

Emblems tell us a great deal about Classic political organisation. The *ahawob* seem to have been independent, although sometimes one lord acknowledged the superior status of another. Yet a glance at a map marking the location of dynastic capitals shows that cities were extraordinarily close to one another, especially in the centre of the Yucatan peninsula. Most lie no more than forty kilometres from their neighbours, suggesting that the average kingdom was small.

Members of the Court

Other people played a large role at court. Among the most central were women. There is good evidence that the wives of rulers were themselves of royal, some-times foreign, birth. Such marriages were surely political: by wedding the daugh-ters of other rulers lords established useful bonds between powerful families and, in the case of struggling or parvenu dynasties, obtained the prestige of older blood lines. Unfortunately, these bonds rarely proved durable.

Also at court, and sometimes at smaller sites nearby, was a group of hereditary nobility, identified by an undeciphered title:

They too attached great importance to legitimate descent. Sometimes their daugh-ters married into royal families, such as happened at Bonampak and Yaxchilan. There is much that is still mysterious, however. Were they cadet branches of the

royal family? Did they have a separate power base in the countryside, as a feudal lord might? Could they form their own kingdom from scratch?

Scribes and sculptors we met in Chapter 2, but there were many other courtly attendants, ranging from musicians to warriors, makers of elaborate costumes, and even dwarfs, who had a special relationship with rulers and their own name glyph:

What did the Classic Élite do?

In the past twenty years our image of the Classic Maya has changed, from that of a tranquil society to a turbulent one ravaged by war and obsessed with blood-letting. It is far too easy, however, to focus on gore and grimness, as some scholars have done. Certainly there was plenty of blood-letting, as well as horrible ways of dispatching captives (skinning, cutting off lips, decapitation, extraction of the heart, pulling of fingernails); but courtly life had other dimensions, including buildings covered with images of flowers, dances using the iridescent plumes of the quetzal bird, enthronement, new year ceremonies, and a rich folklore known from modern Maya and hinted at in glyphs. The society performed rituals with blood, particularly royal blood, because it was a precious and worthy offering, the best the Maya could give, but there was much else for rulers to do.

Consider the most imposing remains of Classic civilisation: stelae, temples and palaces. Through 'dedication verbs' the Maya noted when these were erected and what their names were. One building was called the 'Accession House', another the 'Sweat-bath House'. Stelae too had personal names, as in this example from Caracol, Belize:

A major preoccupation was warfare and the capture of high-ranking warriors. Many conflicts were timed to coincide with momentous junctions of the Venus cycle (such as first appearance as morning star), when warriors would sally forth to battle with enemy dynasties. The glyph identifying these battles includes the sign for Venus:

Such wars could result in profound dynastic crises, especially if rulers were captured.

Rulers and members of the court also engaged in vigorous sports, including a ballgame played within a narrow alley between two parallel structures. The rules of this game are still not well understood. Some sculptures show heavily padded players striking a rubber ball, which must have been unwieldy and bone-crunching as it bounced from player to player across the sloping walls and flat alley of the ballcourt. Players scored points by moving the ball over flat markers on the floor of the court or through rings on the walls. A verb records this event:

Transcription: **pi-tzi-h(a)**

Transliteration: *pitz-ih*

Translation: 'played ball'

At the end of their lives rulers were buried in high style under pyramids, in tombs with jaguar pelts, jade and fine ceramics. Epigraphers have identified the glyph for 'burial':

Transcription: **mu-ka-h(a)/5-?-WITZ**

Transliteration: *muk-ah (ta) ho-?-witz*

Translation: 'was buried (in) the five-?-hill'

These few examples give an idea of the historical richness of Maya glyphs. With only about sixty per cent of the signs deciphered the best and most interesting information is probably yet to come.

A B C D E F G

1

2

3

4

H

1

2

3

4

I1 – N1

O1 – P1

27
Dos Pilas Stela 14,
AD 711.

5
A Sample Text

Not far from the Pasión River, in Guatemala, lies an escarpment with many sites from the Classic period. Among them is Dos Pilas, a ruin that is unusual in northern Guatemala for its relatively untouched condition. Looters have stolen a few monuments (or parts of them) but left intact most of its mounds and pyramids. Heavy jungle growth and the massive roots of mahogany and ceiba trees obscure heaps of collapsed masonry. Here and there the visitor spies a standing wall or lines of stone slabs. Snakes, macaw, puma, howler monkeys and mosquitoes now make this their home.

One temple, really an enormous platform, is at the eastern edge of the site. Its terraces support five stelae, including three in mint condition. Stela 14 shows a ruler, in this case 'Ruler 2', dressed in an elaborate costume. On his head is a bone- or jade-beaded head-dress, over his face a mask. *Oliva* shells and a loincloth – shimmering, to judge from the mirror design – cover his mid-section. To either side of his ankles are a dwarf and a heron. The latter can still be seen diving for fish in the Pasión; dwarfs are in somewhat shorter supply. Under the ruler's feet sprawls a captive.

The text runs as follows:

A1-B4: The Initial Series, of 9 *baktun*, 14 *katun*, 0 *tun*, 0 *uinal* and 0 *kin*; this date corresponds to 5 December AD 711 in our calendar.
A4, C2: The Calendar Round, of 6 Ahau and 13 Muan.
B4-D1: Information about the presiding 'lord of the night'; the age of the current moon (sixteen days in the third lunar half-year)

The sculptor then describes what happened on this date. The ruler, mentioned at F2, erected a stone monument – Stela 14 (E1). This event coincided with the completion of the fourteenth *katun* (D2). The ruler also held the sceptre (E2) while at Dos Pilas (G2).

The secondary texts supplement this basic information. The glyphs above the dwarf refer to two supernaturals, called the 'Paddlers' because they were known to paddle canoes. The text above the captive mentions a Venus war, from which Ruler 2 emerged victorious. The captive, his ear lobes stuffed with cotton swabbing to absorb blood, is named in the brief text at 01-P1.

Stela 14 exemplifies many features of Classic inscriptions: it celebrates the completion of a calendrical cycle; it records the erection of a royal monument and the use of regalia; and it commemorates a battle and the capture of an enemy. The dwarfs, heron and supernaturals suggest more profound matters, not quite spelt out in the text.

Where to see Glyphs

The best place to see glyphs is where they were meant to be seen: at Maya ruins, of which the most accessible are Copan (Honduras), Palenque (Mexico), Quirigua and Tikal (both in Guatemala) and Tonina (Mexico). More remote, but worth a visit for their untouched jungle setting, are the ruins of Yaxchilan (Mexico), Caracol (Belize), Seibal (Guatemala) and Dos Pilas (Guatemala). Most are being excavated or are targeted for excavation. Of the northern sites Chichen Itza (Mexico) has several well-preserved lintels. Less pristine monuments can be seen at Coba (Mexico).

Other texts fall into two categories: those removed by or under agreement with local governments and those stolen from Central America or Mexico for eventual sale to collectors. The following museums and libraries with glyphs are open to the public.

Australia
Canberra, Australian National Gallery
Melbourne, National Gallery of Victoria

Belgium
Brussels, Musées Royaux d'Art et d'Histoire

Belize
Belize City, Bliss Institute
Belmopan, Belize Department of Archaeology

Canada
Toronto, Royal Ontario Museum

Chile
Santiago, Museo Chileno de Arte
 Precolombino

Costa Rica
San José, Instituto Nacional de Seguros

France
Paris, Bibliothèque Nationale
Paris, Musée de l'Homme

Germany (East)
Dresden, Sächsiche Landesbibliothek
 (Dresden Codex)

Germany (West)
Berlin, Museum für Völkerkunde
Cologne, Museum Rautenstrauch-Joest
Freiburg-im-Breisgau, Museum für
 Völkerkunde
Stuttgart, Linden-Museum für Völkerkunde

Guatemala
Flores, Plaza
Guatemala City, Museo Nacional
Guatemala City, Museo Popol Vuh
Santa Elena, Parque de las Estelas
Sayaxche, Alcaldía
Tikal, Museo Sylvanus G. Morley

Honduras
Copan, Museo Arqueológico Copan
Tegucigalpa, Museo Nacional

Israel
Jerusalem, Israel Museum

Mexico
Campeche, Museo de Historia Colonial
Campeche, Museo de Arqueología
Cancún, Museo Regional
Comitán, Casa de las Culturas
Hecelchakan, Museo del Camino Real
Mérida, Museo Regional de Antropología
México, D. F., Museo Nacional de
 Antropología (Grolier Codex in storage)
Oaxaca, Museo de Arte Prehispánico de
 México Rufino Tamayo
Tuxtla Gutierrez, Museo Regional de
 Antropología
Villahermosa, Museo Regional de
 Antropología 'Carlos Pellicer Camera'

Netherlands
Leiden, Rijksmuseum voor Volkenkunde

Spain
Madrid, Museo de América (Madrid Codex)

Sweden
Stockholm, Nationalmuseet

Switzerland
Basle, Museum für Völkerkunde

UK
London, Museum of Mankind (British
  Museum)

USA
Cambridge, Peabody Museum, Harvard
  University
Chicago, Art Institute
Chicago, Field Museum of Natural History
Cleveland, Cleveland Museum of Art
Dallas, Museum of Fine Arts
Denver, Denver Art Museum
Denver, Denver Museum of Natural History
Detroit, Detroit Institute of Art

Fort Worth, Kimbell Art Museum
Houston, De Menil Collection
Houston, Houston Museum of Fine Arts
Kansas City, Nelson Gallery-Atkins Museum
Los Angeles, Los Angeles County Museum of
  Art
New Haven, Yale University Art Gallery
New Orleans, New Orleans Museum of Art
New York, American Museum of Natural
  History
New York, Metropolitan Museum of Art
New York, Museum of the American Indian,
  Heye Foundation
Philadelphia, University Museum
Princeton, Princeton University Art Museum
Redlands, San Bernardino County Museum
Rockford, Time Museum
St Louis, St Louis Museum of Art
Washington, Dumbarton Oaks

Bibliographical Note

The literature on Maya glyphs is vast and specialised. Still the most comprehensive source is J.E.S. Thompson, *Maya Hieroglyphic Writing* (Norman, 1973), which, regrettably, is now dated in its conclusions and dauntingly encyclopedic for the beginner. The same can be said of D. Kelley, *Deciphering the Mayan Script* (Austin, 1976), the other standard reference work, which none the less contains a superb treatment of Maya epigraphy and its development. A more accessible study is L. Schele and M. Miller, *Blood of Kings* (Fort Worth, 1986), which places new decipherments in an interpretation of their cultural context. The thesis of the book, that royal blood-letting formed the corner-stone of Maya society, is controversial and should be compared with the strictly grammatical approach of V. Bricker, *Grammar of Mayan Hieroglyphs* (New Orleans, 1986). A good sample of recent opinion appears in J. Justeson, and L. Campbell (eds), *Phoneticism in Mayan Hieroglyphic Writing* (Albany, 1984) and in a chapter by J. Fox in S. Morley, G. Brainerd and R. Sharer, *The Ancient Maya* (Stanford, 1983). An excellent series of research reports on individual decipherments is now being published by the Center for Maya Research in Washington, D.C. For a more general introduction to the Maya the reader should consult either M. Coe's *The Maya* (London, 1987) or N. Hammond's *Ancient Maya Civilization* (Cambridge, 1982).

There are almost 5,000 Maya texts, including those on pottery, but only a few are published to a satisfactory standard. For stone monuments I. Graham, *Corpus of Maya Hieroglyphic Inscriptions* (Cambridge, Mass.), now in its fourteenth tome, remains the definitive source, although it is many years from completion. Fuller commentary appears in C. Jones and L. Satterthwaite, *Monuments and Inscriptions of Tikal* (Philadelphia, 1982), a model of reporting on a single site. Several publications, including M. Coe, *The Maya Scribe and his World* (New York, 1973), illustrate texts on pottery; however, the reader should be warned that some such hieroglyphs are unreliable, having been heavily and imaginatively restored.

Index